I Can't Handle Me Any Kind of Way

Why Self-Care Is Essential to Your Mind, Body, and Spirit"

By

Vanita Patterson

"Coping with Myself: A Journey to Balance"

In the hustle and bustle of our modern lives, it's easy to lose ourselves in the chaos. We are constantly bombarded with responsibilities, expectations, and the demands of a fast-paced world. In this relentless pursuit of success and fulfillment, we often neglect the most important aspect of our existence: ourselves. "I can't handle me in any kind of way," is a sentiment shared by many, and it underscores the critical need for self-care. This book delves into the profound importance of self-care for the well-being of our mind, body, and spirit, exploring its various dimensions and offering practical insights for integrating self-care into our lives.

The Neglected Self

"I can't handle me." These words echo the experiences of countless individuals who have felt overwhelmed by the challenges of life. It's a declaration of vulnerability, an acknowledgment of our own limitations when we neglect self-care. In a world that often celebrates busyness and achievement, taking a step back to care for ourselves can feel like an indulgence we can't afford. However, as we explore the depths of self-care, we begin to understand that it's not an indulgence yet a necessity.

Mind, the Seat of Our Thoughts

Our mind, a complex and powerful organ, is the seat of our thoughts, emotions, and consciousness. Neglecting its care can lead to a cascade of detrimental effects on our overall well-being. Stress, anxiety, and burnout are just a few of the consequences of a mind left unattended. In our fast-paced world, the importance of nurturing our mental health cannot be overstated. Self-care provides the tools to do just that.

Body, the Temple We Inhabit

Our bodies are the vessels through which we experience life. Neglecting our physical well-being can have profound consequences. From chronic illnesses to the subtle erosion of vitality, the toll of disregarding our bodies is high. Self-care offers a path to reconnection with our physical selves. It reminds us to nourish our bodies with wholesome nutrition, invigorate them through movement, and grant them the rest they need to rejuvenate.

Spirit, the Essence of Being

Beyond the mind and body lies the realm of the spirit; an elusive and deeply personal aspect of our existence. It's the essence of our being, the source of our values, and the wellspring of our inner strength. Without tending to our spiritual needs, we risk feeling disconnected, purposeless, and adrift in life. Self-care allows us to explore and cultivate our spirituality, whether through mindfulness practices, meditation, or simply immersing ourselves in the awe-inspiring beauty of the natural world.

The Multidimensional Nature of Self-Care

Self-care is not a one-size-fits-all concept. It's a multidimensional approach to nurturing every facet of our being. Physical self-care involves the choices we make to maintain our bodies, while emotional self-care hones our ability to navigate the complex terrain of our feelings. Social self-care underscores the importance of healthy relationships, and intellectual self-care encourages continuous learning and mental stimulation. Creative self-care taps into our inner well of creativity, enabling self-expression and the exploration of our passions.

The Role of Self-Care in Mental Health

The intimate connection between self-care and mental health cannot be overstated. Neglecting self-care can lead to burnout, anxiety, depression, and a host of other mental health challenges. However, when we prioritize self-care, we equip ourselves with the tools to manage stress, build emotional resilience, and promote mental well-being. Self-care becomes a lifeline in turbulent times, a means of nurturing our minds back to health.

Conclusion

"I can't handle me in any kind of way" is a stark reminder of the consequences of neglecting self-care. Yet, it also serves as a rallying cry to reclaim our well-being. Self-care is not a luxury reserved for those with ample free time; it is an essential practice that empowers us to lead fulfilling lives. As we embark on this exploration of self-care, we uncover the profound interconnectedness of our mind, body, and spirit. It is a journey of rediscovering ourselves and forging a path toward a balanced, harmonious existence. In the chapters that follow, we will delve deeper into the various dimensions of self-care and offer practical guidance for integrating it into our lives.

Contents

Chapter 1: Defining Self-Care

1.1 What Is Self-Care?

- Understanding the concept of self-care.
- Differentiating self-care from self-indulgence.
- The history and evolution of self-care practices.

1.2 The Importance of Self-Care

- Highlighting the consequences of neglecting self-care.
- How self-care enhances the overall quality of life.
- Recognizing the role of self-care in mental health.

Defining Self-Care

In a world that often glorifies productivity and self-sacrifice, the concept of self-care has gained significant attention and importance in recent years. While it may seem like a trendy buzzword, self-care is a fundamental aspect of maintaining a healthy, balanced life. In this chapter, we will explore the multifaceted concept of self-care, understanding its essence, distinguishing it from self-indulgence, and delving into the historical evolution of self-care practices.

1.1 What Is Self-Care?

Understanding the Concept of Self-Care

Self-care is a holistic approach to nurturing and preserving one's physical, emotional, mental, and spiritual well-being. It encompasses a wide range of activities, practices, and habits that individuals engage in to promote self-preservation, personal growth, and overall health. Self-care is not limited to just one aspect of our lives; it addresses our entire being, recognizing the interconnectedness of our mind, body, and spirit.

Self-care involves activities that allow individuals to prioritize their own well-being and recharge their physical and emotional batteries. It is not a one-size-fits-all concept, as what constitutes self-care can vary greatly from person to person. For some, it may involve exercise and physical health maintenance, while for others, it might be more focused on relaxation and mental well-being.

Differentiating Self-Care from Self-Indulgence

One common misconception about self-care is that it is synonymous with self-indulgence. While both concepts involve taking care of oneself, they differ significantly in their underlying principles and motivations.

Self-indulgence often implies excessive or uncontrolled gratification of one's desires and impulses. It can involve behaviors that may provide momentary pleasure but do not necessarily contribute to long-term well-being. For example, overindulging in unhealthy foods or excessive spending on luxury items might be considered self-indulgent.

On the other hand, self-care is a deliberate and conscious act of self-preservation and improvement. It entails making choices that promote physical and mental health, reduce stress, and enhance one's overall quality of life. Self-care activities are grounded in self-awareness and a genuine desire for self-improvement and well-being.

It is crucial to recognize that self-care is not selfish. Engaging in self-care activities allows individuals to be more present, energetic, and effective in their roles as parents, partners, friends, and professionals. When we take care of ourselves, we are better equipped to care for others.

The History and Evolution of Self-Care Practices

The concept of self-care is not a recent phenomenon; it has evolved over centuries and across cultures. The roots of self-care can be traced back to ancient civilizations, where various practices were developed to promote physical and mental well-being.

Ancient Traditions: In ancient Greece, the practice of "philautia" or self-love, was highly regarded. Greek philosophers emphasized the importance of taking care of oneself as a foundation for contributing positively to society. Similarly, ancient Chinese medicine and Ayurveda in India incorporated self-care practices that involved balance and harmony of the body and mind.

Medieval Europe: During the Middle Ages in Europe, monastic traditions and religious orders often prescribed periods of self-care, including meditation, prayer, and solitude, to foster spiritual growth and inner peace.

Industrial Revolution: The advent of the Industrial Revolution in the 18th and 19th centuries brought about significant changes in work patterns and lifestyles. It also led to the recognition of the importance of rest and leisure as a form of self-care to counter the negative effects of labor-intensive, industrial work.

20th Century: In the 20th century, psychology and mental health practices began to incorporate self-care concepts into therapy and counseling. Self-help books and the rise of the wellness industry further popularized self-care practices.

Today, self-care has become a mainstream concept, with countless books, articles, and social media influencers promoting various self-care strategies. However, despite its widespread acknowledgment, many individuals still struggle to integrate self-care into their lives effectively.

1.2 The Importance of Self-Care

Highlighting the Consequences of Neglecting Self-Care

Neglecting self-care can have significant consequences on both our physical and mental well-being. In our fast-paced, modern world, it is not uncommon for individuals to prioritize work, family, and other obligations over their own self-care. Over time, this can lead to burnout, chronic stress, and various physical and psychological ailments.

Burnout: The World Health Organization officially recognized burnout as an occupational phenomenon in 2019. Burnout is characterized by emotional exhaustion, reduced performance, and feelings of cynicism or detachment from work. It is often a result of prolonged neglect of self-care and the relentless pursuit of productivity.

Chronic Stress: Neglecting self-care can lead to chronic stress, which has a detrimental impact on both mental and physical health. Chronic stress is associated with conditions such as anxiety, depression, cardiovascular disease, and weakened immune function.

Reduced Quality of Life: A lack of self-care can diminish one's overall quality of life. Individuals who consistently put their well-being on the backburner may find themselves feeling unfulfilled, disconnected, and constantly fatigued.

How Self-Care Enhances Overall Quality of Life

On the flip side, actively practicing self-care can significantly enhance one's quality of life. When individuals prioritize self-care, they experience a range of benefits that positively impact various aspects of their existence:

Improved Physical Health: Engaging in regular exercise, maintaining a balanced diet, getting adequate sleep, and managing stress through self-care practices contribute to better physical health. These habits can reduce the risk of chronic diseases, increase energy levels, and improve overall vitality.

Enhanced Mental Well-Being: Self-care activities like mindfulness meditation, journaling, and seeking therapy can improve mental health by reducing symptoms of anxiety, depression, and stress. They promote emotional resilience, self-awareness, and a greater sense of control over one's emotions.

Greater Emotional Resilience: Self-care activities that focus on emotional well-being, such as setting boundaries, practicing self-compassion, and seeking support from friends or professionals, build emotional resilience. This resilience helps individuals navigate life's challenges with greater ease and adaptability.

Improved Relationships: When individuals practice self-care, they are better equipped to cultivate healthy relationships. By understanding and meeting their own needs, they can offer more to their loved ones, fostering stronger and more fulfilling connections.

Increased Productivity and Creativity: Self-care can enhance cognitive function, creativity, and problem-solving abilities. Taking breaks, engaging in hobbies, and finding time for relaxation can lead to increased productivity and a more creative approach to life's challenges.

Recognizing the Role of Self-Care in Mental Health

Mental health is a vital component of overall well-being, and self-care plays a crucial role in maintaining and improving it. Mental health conditions, such as anxiety and depression, are widespread, affecting millions of people worldwide. Recognizing the significance of self-care in mental health is paramount.

Preventing Mental Health Challenges: Engaging in self-care practices can be a proactive measure to prevent the onset of mental health challenges. By managing stress, building emotional resilience, and nurturing one's mental well-being, individuals can reduce their vulnerability to conditions like anxiety and depression.

Managing Existing Mental Health Conditions: For individuals already living with mental health conditions, self-care is an essential part of their treatment and recovery. It can complement therapeutic interventions and medication by providing tools and strategies for coping with symptoms and improving overall mental health.

Reducing Stigma: Embracing self-care as a standard practice can contribute to reducing the stigma associated with mental health issues. When self-care is openly discussed and prioritized, it sends a message that taking care of one's mental health is a normal and commendable aspect of life.

In summary, self-care is far more than a fleeting trend; it is a vital component of a healthy and balanced life. Understanding its essence, distinguishing it from self-indulgence, and recognizing its historical evolution are crucial steps in incorporating self-care practices into our daily routines. The consequences of neglecting self-care are significant, but the benefits of prioritizing it extend to physical health, mental well-being, and overall quality of life. Moreover, self-care plays a pivotal role in preventing and managing mental health conditions, ultimately contributing to a happier and more fulfilling life.

Chapter 2: The Mind-Body Connection

2.1 Mind and Body: A Unified System

- Exploring the interconnectedness of mental and physical health.
- The impact of stress on the mind and body.
- The mind's role in physical healing.

2.2 Stress Management and Self-Care

- Strategies for reducing stress through self-care.
- The relationship between chronic stress and physical ailments.
- Mindfulness and meditation as tools for mind-body balance.

The Mind-Body Connection

In the intricate dance of human existence, the mind and body are not separate entities but integral parts of a unified system. This profound interconnectedness forms the foundation of our well-being and shapes our experiences in ways that are both fascinating and undeniable. The intricate relationship between our mental and physical health underscores the critical need to explore the mind-body connection comprehensively. In this chapter, we embark on a journey to unravel the mysteries of this connection, seeking to understand how these two fundamental aspects of our existence are intricately linked.

The mind is not an isolated entity confined to our thoughts and emotions; it exerts a profound influence on the body it inhabits. Conversely, our physical state significantly impacts our mental well-being. This dynamic interaction between the mind and body manifests in various ways, shaping our daily lives and experiences.

As we explore the depths of the mind-body connection, we will unearth its implications for our overall health and quality of life. One critical aspect we will delve into is the impact of stress, a common and pervasive element of modern life, on both our mental and physical well-being. Chronic stress, in particular, takes a toll on our mind and body that cannot be ignored. Stress management, grounded in self-care practices, emerges as a vital component of maintaining a harmonious mind-body relationship.

Throughout this chapter, we will navigate the intricate pathways that link our mental and physical realms. We will uncover the ways in which our emotions and thoughts reverberate through our bodies, shaping our health and experiences. We will also delve into the physical manifestations of stress, understanding how chronic stress can lead to a cascade of health issues.

Moreover, we will explore the mind's remarkable role in the process of physical healing. The power of belief, as exemplified by the placebo effect, illustrates how the mind can influence our bodies' responses and capacity for recovery. We will discover how mind-body healing techniques, such as meditation and guided imagery, offer valuable tools for enhancing our overall well-being.

As we proceed, we will emphasize the profound implications of this mind-body connection for our daily lives. It underscores the importance of nurturing both our mental and physical health, recognizing that they are intertwined aspects of our being. Additionally, we will underscore the critical need for effective stress management, which is an integral part of self-care, to safeguard our mind and body against the detrimental effects of chronic stress.

Ultimately, by delving into the mind-body connection and the impact of stress on our well-being, we gain valuable insights into the intricate web of our existence. Armed with this understanding, we are better equipped to make informed choices and engage in self-care practices that harmonize the complex interplay between our mental and physical health.

2.1 Mind and Body: A Unified System

Exploring the Interconnectedness of Mental and Physical Health

The prevailing paradigm often separates mental health from physical health, as if they exist in isolation. However, the truth is that they are deeply interwoven, influencing each other in profound ways. Our emotions, thoughts, and mental states have a direct impact on our physical well-being, and vice versa.

Emotions and the Body: Emotions are not just fleeting mental states; they manifest in the body as well. When we experience joy, our bodies respond with smiles and laughter, while anger can trigger increased heart rate and muscle tension. Chronic negative emotions like stress and anxiety can lead to physical ailments, from tension headaches to digestive problems.

The Body's Influence on the Mind: Conversely, the state of our physical health can profoundly affect our mental state. Chronic pain, for example, can lead to depression, and a lack of physical activity can contribute to feelings of lethargy and sadness. The brain is intimately connected to the body, and its functioning depends on the health of the body's systems.

The Impact of Stress on the Mind and Body

Stress is a natural response to challenging situations, and in small doses, it can be beneficial, motivating us to take action and stay alert. However, chronic stress is a different beast altogether. Prolonged exposure to stress can wreak havoc on both our mental and physical health.

Mental Health Implications: Chronic stress is a leading contributor to mental health issues such as anxiety and depression. It can lead to persistent feelings of overwhelm, irritability, and a sense of hopelessness. The constant activation of the body's stress response system can also impair cognitive function, making it difficult to concentrate and make clear decisions.

Physical Health Consequences: The physical toll of chronic stress is significant. It can contribute to a wide range of physical ailments, including cardiovascular disease, digestive problems, and weakened immune function. Stress can exacerbate existing health conditions and slow down the body's natural healing processes.

The Mind's Role in Physical Healing

While we often think of medical treatments as primarily addressing the physical body, the mind plays a substantial role in the healing process. The mind-body connection is evident in the placebo effect, where individuals experience real improvements in their physical conditions when they believe they are receiving treatment, even if the treatment is inert.

The Placebo Effect: The placebo effect underscores the power of the mind in influencing physical outcomes. Belief in the efficacy of a treatment can activate the body's natural healing mechanisms, leading to reduced pain, improved symptoms, and faster recovery.

Mind-Body Healing Techniques: Beyond the placebo effect, various mind-body healing techniques have gained recognition for their efficacy. These practices, which include meditation, guided imagery, and relaxation exercises, harness the mind's ability to influence the body positively. They are often used in conjunction with medical treatments to enhance healing and improve overall well-being.

2.2 Stress Management and Self-Care

Strategies for Reducing Stress Through Self-Care

Given the profound impact of chronic stress on both the mind and body, it is crucial to develop effective strategies for stress management. Self-care plays a central role in mitigating stress and promoting overall well-being.

Physical Self-Care: Engaging in regular physical activity is one of the most effective ways to combat stress. Exercise releases endorphins, the body's natural stress relievers, and promotes a sense of well-being. Adequate sleep and proper nutrition also play essential roles in stress management.

Emotional Self-Care: Managing stress involves recognizing and addressing our emotional responses to challenging situations. Practices like journaling, seeking therapy or counseling, and practicing self-compassion can help individuals navigate their emotions in healthy ways.

Social Self-Care: Healthy relationships are a source of support and resilience in times of stress. Maintaining strong social connections, setting boundaries, and seeking support from loved ones are critical aspects of social self-care.

Intellectual Self-Care: Mental stimulation and continuous learning can help keep stress at bay. Engaging in intellectually stimulating activities, setting achievable goals, and balancing mental challenges with relaxation are essential for intellectual self-care.

Creative Self-Care: Engaging in creative pursuits can be a powerful antidote to stress. Creative activities, whether painting, writing, or playing music, provide an outlet for self-expression and a means of relaxation.

The Relationship Between Chronic Stress and Physical Ailments

Chronic stress is not merely a mental burden; it exacts a tangible toll on the body. Understanding the links between stress and physical health is crucial for appreciating the significance of stress management through self-care.

Cardiovascular Health: Chronic stress can lead to high blood pressure, which is a significant risk factor for heart disease and stroke. It also contributes to the narrowing of arteries, increasing the likelihood of heart attacks.

Digestive System: Stress can disrupt the normal functioning of the digestive system, leading to conditions like irritable bowel syndrome (IBS), gastritis, and acid reflux.

Immune Function: Prolonged stress weakens the immune system, making the body more susceptible to infections and illnesses. It can also slow down the healing process.

Chronic Pain: Stress can exacerbate chronic pain conditions such as migraines, fibromyalgia, and arthritis. It can also increase the perception of pain.

Mindfulness and Meditation as Tools for Mind-Body Balance

In recent years, mindfulness and meditation have gained widespread recognition as effective tools for reducing stress and promoting mind-body balance. These practices involve cultivating present-moment awareness and can have profound effects on both mental and physical health.

Stress Reduction: Mindfulness and meditation techniques encourage individuals to observe their thoughts and emotions without judgment. This non-reactive awareness can help reduce the impact of stressors and promote a sense of calm and equanimity.

Improved Mental Health: Regular mindfulness and meditation practice have been shown to reduce symptoms of anxiety and depression. They can enhance emotional regulation and foster a greater sense of well-being.

Physical Benefits: Mindfulness and meditation practices are associated with reduced blood pressure, improved immune function, and enhanced cardiovascular health. They can also alleviate symptoms of chronic pain conditions.

Enhanced Mind-Body Connection: Mindfulness and meditation strengthen the mind-body connection, helping individuals become more attuned to their bodies and better able to respond to physical and emotional cues.

In conclusion, the mind-body connection is a fundamental aspect of our existence, with mental and physical health intricately intertwined. Chronic stress can have profound consequences on both our mental and physical well-being, making effective stress management crucial. Self-care practices, spanning physical, emotional, social, intellectual, and creative dimensions, offer powerful tools for reducing stress and promoting overall well-being. Additionally, mindfulness and meditation, with their ability to foster mind-body balance, provide valuable means of enhancing mental and physical health. As we delve deeper into the exploration of self-care, we will uncover more strategies and insights to nurture our mind, body, and spirit.

Chapter 3: The Spirituality of Self-Care

3.1 Nurturing the Spirit

- Defining spirituality in a secular context.

- How self-care can support and enhance one's spiritual journey.

- Exploring various spiritual practices within self-care.

3.2 Self-Reflection and Inner Growth

- The role of self-reflection in spiritual development.

- Mindful self-care as a path to self-discovery.

- Balancing inner and outer worlds through self-care.

The Spirituality of Self-Care

In a world that often emphasizes the material and the tangible, the realm of spirituality offers a different perspective—an exploration of the intangible, the transcendental, and the deeply personal. The journey of self-care is not merely confined to the physical and mental aspects of our being; it extends into the realm of the spiritual. In this chapter, we will delve into the spirituality of self-care, understanding its significance within a secular context, and how it can enrich our lives. We will explore various spiritual practices that seamlessly merge with self-care, fostering a profound sense of inner peace, purpose, and connection.

3.1 Nurturing the Spirit

Defining Spirituality in a Secular Context

Spirituality is a concept that often carries religious connotations. However, in a secular context, spirituality refers to the deeply personal quest for meaning, purpose, and connection in life. It is not bound by religious doctrines but encompasses a wide spectrum of beliefs, values, and practices that speak to the human spirit. Spirituality acknowledges the existence of something greater than ourselves, whether it's a connection to nature, a sense of universal consciousness, or an exploration of inner wisdom.

In the secular realm, spirituality invites individuals to explore the questions that transcend the material world: Who am I? What is my purpose? How do I find meaning in life? It encourages a journey of self-discovery and connection with something larger than oneself, whether that's through personal beliefs, values, or the recognition of the interconnectedness of all life.

How Self-Care Can Support and Enhance One's Spiritual Journey

Self-care and spirituality are not separate paths; they are intertwined facets of holistic well-being. Self-care practices provide the foundation upon which spiritual growth can flourish. Here's how self-care can support and enhance one's spiritual journey:

Inner Peace: Self-care practices, such as meditation and mindfulness, cultivate inner peace, creating a fertile ground for spiritual exploration. A calm and centered mind is more receptive to moments of insight and transcendence.

Self-Reflection: Self-care encourages self-reflection, allowing individuals to delve into the depths of their consciousness. This introspection is a vital aspect of spiritual development, as it leads to greater self-awareness and understanding.

Mind-Body-Spirit Connection: The holistic approach of self-care recognizes the interconnectedness of mind, body, and spirit. It honors the importance of nurturing the spiritual aspect of our being alongside the physical and mental dimensions.

Alignment with Values: Engaging in self-care practices that align with one's values and beliefs fosters a sense of authenticity and purpose. This alignment deepens the spiritual connection to one's inner compass.

Connection to Others: Self-care extends beyond individual practices to include nurturing relationships and social connections. These connections can offer support and shared spiritual experiences, fostering a sense of belonging and interconnectedness.

Exploring Various Spiritual Practices within Self-Care

Spirituality finds expression in myriad practices, each offering a unique path to self-discovery and connection. Within the realm of self-care, several spiritual practices seamlessly merge, enriching our inner lives. Here are some examples:

Meditation: Meditation is a cornerstone of many spiritual traditions. It encourages stillness of the mind, enabling individuals to tap into their inner wisdom and experience moments of transcendence. Regular meditation practice is a form of self-care that nurtures the spirit.

Mindfulness: Mindfulness, rooted in Buddhist philosophy, involves being fully present in the moment. It deepens our connection to life as it unfolds and enhances our awareness of the interconnectedness of all beings.

Yoga: Yoga, an ancient practice originating in India, combines physical postures, breath control, and meditation. It promotes physical health while fostering a sense of spiritual awakening and unity with the universe.

Nature Connection: For many, the natural world is a profound source of spiritual inspiration. Spending time in nature, whether through hiking, gardening or simply contemplating a beautiful sunset, can be a form of self-care that nurtures the spirit.

Journaling: Keeping a journal allows individuals to explore their thoughts, feelings, and beliefs. It is a powerful tool for self-reflection and can aid in the development of a deeper spiritual understanding.

3.2 Self-Reflection and Inner Growth

The Role of Self-Reflection in Spiritual Development

Self-reflection is a fundamental aspect of spiritual development. It involves looking inward, examining our thoughts, emotions, and beliefs, and seeking to understand our place in the grand tapestry of existence. Self-care practices provide the ideal platform for self-reflection, offering moments of quiet introspection and the opportunity to explore the deeper aspects of our inner world.

Self-Discovery: Through self-reflection, individuals embark on a journey of self-discovery. They uncover their core values, beliefs, and desires, gaining insight into what truly matters to them.

Alignment with Values: Self-reflection helps individuals align their actions with their values, fostering a sense of authenticity and purpose. It encourages a harmonious integration of one's beliefs into everyday life.

Emotional Healing: Delving into the recesses of one's psyche can lead to emotional healing. Self-reflection allows individuals to address unresolved emotional wounds, cultivate self-compassion, and foster emotional resilience.

Enhanced Relationships: Self-reflection deepens our understanding of ourselves and others. It promotes empathy, compassion, and the ability to communicate more effectively in our relationships, contributing to a more profound sense of interconnectedness.

Mindful Self-Care as a Path to Self-Discovery

Mindful self-care is a potent combination of self-care practices and mindfulness—a state of heightened awareness of the present moment without judgment. It offers a path to self-discovery and inner growth by nurturing the mind, body, and spirit simultaneously.

Presence: Mindful self-care encourages individuals to be fully present in their self-care activities, whether it's eating a nourishing meal, going for a walk, or engaging in a creative pursuit. This presence fosters a deeper connection to the experience and enhances self-awareness.

Self-Compassion: Mindfulness practices within self-care also promote self-compassion. Individuals learn to treat themselves with kindness and understanding, just as they would a dear friend. This self-compassion is an essential aspect of spiritual growth, as it invites a gentle and accepting attitude toward oneself.

Integration: Mindful self-care encourages the integration of spiritual values into daily life. Whether it's infusing gratitude into morning routines or finding moments of stillness in a busy day, these practices promote the alignment of one's spiritual beliefs with their actions.

Balancing Inner and Outer Worlds through Self-Care

A holistic approach to self-care involves balancing the inner and outer worlds. While self-care encompasses activities that promote physical health and mental well-being, it also includes practices that nourish the spirit and foster a sense of inner peace.

Outer Self-Care: This aspect of self-care includes physical activities such as exercise, nutrition, and sleep, as well as mental practices like stress management and relaxation techniques. It ensures that the body and mind are well cared for and in optimal condition.

Inner Self-Care: Inner self-care is the domain of the spirit. It involves practices like meditation, mindfulness, and journaling that nurture the inner world. These practices provide the spiritual nourishment necessary for a sense of meaning, purpose, and connection.

Balanced Well-Being: The balance between inner and outer self-care leads to a more balanced state of overall well-being. When individuals tend to both their physical and spiritual needs, they experience a greater sense of wholeness and harmony in their lives.

In conclusion, the spirituality of self-care invites us to explore the deeper dimensions of our existence. It defines spirituality within a secular context, acknowledging the personal quest for meaning and connection. Self-care seamlessly merges with spirituality, offering a path to inner peace, purpose, and self-discovery. Self-reflection plays a central role in spiritual development, fostering self-awareness and alignment with one's values. Mindful self-care combines self-care practices with mindfulness, nurturing the mind, body, and spirit. Ultimately, by embracing the spirituality of self-care and cultivating a harmonious balance between inner and outer well-being, individuals can embark on a profound journey of inner growth, connection, and self-discovery.

Chapter 4: Self-Care Practices

4.1 Physical Self-Care

- The significance of physical well-being.
- Exercise, nutrition, and sleep as pillars of physical self-care.
- Overcoming barriers to maintaining physical health.

4.2 Emotional Self-Care

- Understanding and managing emotions.
- The importance of seeking support and therapy.
- Cultivating emotional resilience through self-care.

4.3 Social Self-Care

- The role of relationships in our well-being.
- Setting boundaries and fostering healthy connections.
- The impact of social self-care on mental health.

4.4 Intellectual Self-Care

- Nourishing the mind through continuous learning.
- The connection between intellectual stimulation and emotional well-being.
- Balancing mental challenges with relaxation.

4.5 Creative Self-Care

- Unleashing creativity as a form of self-expression.

- The therapeutic benefits of artistic pursuits.
- Finding inspiration in everyday life.

Self-Care Practices

Self-care is not a one-size-fits-all concept; it's a multifaceted approach to nurturing every aspect of your being—physical, emotional, social, intellectual, and creative. In this chapter, we will delve into the various dimensions of self-care and explore practical self-care practices that empower you to take charge of your well-being.

4.1 Physical Self-Care

The Significance of Physical Well-Being

Physical well-being is the foundation upon which all other dimensions of self-care rest. A healthy body provides the energy and vitality needed to engage fully in life. Physical self-care encompasses practices that promote physical health and resilience.

Exercise: Regular physical activity is essential for maintaining physical health. Exercise not only keeps your body in shape but also releases endorphins, the body's natural mood lifters. Whether it's a brisk walk, yoga, weightlifting, or dancing, find an activity you enjoy and make it a part of your routine.

Nutrition: Proper nutrition fuels your body and mind. A balanced diet rich in fruits, vegetables, lean proteins, and whole grains provides the nutrients needed for optimal functioning. Avoid excessive processed foods, sugary drinks, and unhealthy snacks.

Sleep: Quality sleep is crucial for physical and mental well-being. Establish a regular sleep schedule and create a sleep-conducive environment. Aim for 7-9 hours of restful sleep each night to support physical recovery and cognitive function.

Overcoming Barriers to Maintaining Physical Health

While physical self-care is essential, many people face barriers that make it challenging to prioritize their physical well-being. Common obstacles include a busy schedule, lack of motivation, or health issues. Overcoming these barriers requires commitment and tailored strategies:

Time Management: Schedule physical activity as you would any other appointment. Treat it as a non-negotiable part of your day to ensure consistency.

Motivation: Find activities you genuinely enjoy to make exercise more appealing. Consider working out with a friend or hiring a personal trainer for added motivation.

Health Issues: If you have specific health concerns, consult with a healthcare professional for guidance on suitable exercise and dietary modifications. They can help you create a plan tailored to your needs.

4.2 Emotional Self-Care

Understanding and Managing Emotions

Emotions are an integral part of the human experience. Emotional self-care involves recognizing, understanding, and managing your emotions in healthy ways. This dimension of self-care is crucial for emotional well-being and resilience.

Self-Awareness: Begin by developing self-awareness. Pay attention to your emotions and their triggers. Journaling can be a helpful tool for tracking your emotional responses and identifying patterns.

Emotional Regulation: Learn strategies to regulate your emotions effectively. Techniques such as deep breathing, progressive muscle relaxation, and mindfulness can help you stay calm and centered in challenging situations.

Seeking Support: Don't hesitate to seek support when needed. Talking to a therapist or counselor can provide a safe space to explore and process your emotions. Professional support can be particularly beneficial when dealing with complex emotional issues or trauma.

The Importance of Seeking Support and Therapy

Therapy or counseling is a valuable form of emotional self-care that allows individuals to address a wide range of emotional challenges. Some reasons to seek therapy include:

Mental Health Conditions: Therapy can provide effective treatment for conditions such as depression, anxiety, and post-traumatic stress disorder.

Stress Management: Therapists can teach stress management techniques and coping strategies to deal with life's challenges.

Grief and Loss: Therapy offers support and guidance when dealing with grief and loss, helping individuals navigate the complex emotions associated with these experiences.

Relationship Issues: Couples therapy and family therapy can improve communication and relationships, fostering healthier connections.

Self-Exploration: Therapy provides an opportunity for self-exploration and personal growth, helping individuals gain insight into their thoughts, feelings, and behaviors.

Cultivating Emotional Resilience through Self-Care

Emotional resilience is the ability to adapt and bounce back from adversity. It's a key component of emotional self-care and involves developing coping skills and a positive mindset.

Mindfulness and Meditation: These practices cultivate mindfulness, which allows you to observe your thoughts and emotions without judgment. This can reduce emotional reactivity and improve emotional regulation.

Self-Compassion: Treat yourself with the same kindness and understanding you would offer to a friend. Self-compassion involves acknowledging your imperfections and failures without harsh self-criticism.

Healthy Coping Strategies: Replace unhealthy coping mechanisms (e.g., substance abuse or avoidance) with healthier alternatives like exercise, creative expression, or seeking support from friends and family.

Developing Resilience: Embrace challenges as opportunities for growth. Building resilience involves reframing negative experiences and developing a mindset that views setbacks as valuable learning experiences.

4.3 Social Self-Care

The Role of Relationships in Our Well-Being

Human beings are inherently social creatures, and our connections with others play a significant role in our overall well-being. Social self-care involves nurturing healthy relationships, setting boundaries, and fostering a support network.

Healthy Connections: Cultivate meaningful and supportive relationships with friends, family, and loved ones. These connections provide emotional support, companionship, and a sense of belonging.

Boundaries: Establish and maintain healthy boundaries in your relationships. Clearly communicate your needs, values, and limits to ensure that your well-being is respected.

Isolation vs. Socialization: Balance solitude and social interaction according to your needs. While spending time alone can be restorative, maintaining social connections is vital for emotional health.

Setting Boundaries and Fostering Healthy Connections

Setting boundaries is a fundamental aspect of social self-care. Boundaries define the limits of acceptable behavior and protect your emotional well-being. Here are some steps to establish and maintain healthy boundaries:

Identify Your Needs: Reflect on your emotional needs and what makes you comfortable or uncomfortable in relationships. Awareness of your needs is the first step in setting boundaries.

Communicate Clearly: Clearly express your boundaries to others in a respectful and assertive manner. Use "I" statements to convey your feelings and expectations.

Consistency: Consistently enforce your boundaries. This sends a message that you value and respect your well-being.

Respect Others' Boundaries: Remember that boundaries are a two-way street. Respect others' boundaries as you expect them to respect yours.

Seek Support: If you struggle with boundary setting, consider seeking support from a therapist or counselor who can provide guidance and strategies.

The Impact of Social Self-Care on Mental Health

Social self-care has a profound impact on mental health. Maintaining healthy relationships and social connections offers several mental health benefits:

Emotional Support: Friends and loved ones provide emotional support during challenging times, reducing feelings of loneliness and isolation.

Stress Reduction: Social interactions and shared experiences can reduce stress levels and improve overall well-being.

Sense of Belonging: Belonging to a community or social group fosters a sense of purpose and belonging, contributing to positive mental health.

Improved Coping: Social connections can enhance coping skills, helping individuals navigate life's ups and downs more effectively.

4.4 Intellectual Self-Care

Nourishing the Mind Through Continuous Learning

Intellectual self-care focuses on nurturing your mind through learning, growth, and mental stimulation. It acknowledges the importance of intellectual well-being for overall life satisfaction.

Continuous Learning: Engage in lifelong learning. Whether it's formal education, reading, taking up a new hobby, or pursuing a skill, the act of learning keeps the mind active and engaged.

Curiosity: Cultivate curiosity about the world around you. Ask questions, explore new topics, and seek out opportunities for intellectual growth.

Challenging Yourself: Challenge your mental abilities regularly. Solve puzzles, engage in critical thinking exercises, or take on projects that require problem-solving.

The Connection Between Intellectual Stimulation and Emotional Well-Being

Intellectual self-care is closely linked to emotional well-being. Engaging in intellectually stimulating activities can have a positive impact on your emotional health in several ways:

Mental Resilience: Intellectual challenges can enhance mental resilience, making it easier to cope with stress and adversity.

Increased Self-Esteem: Accomplishing intellectual goals or acquiring new knowledge can boost self-esteem and self-confidence.

Emotional Regulation: Engaging in intellectual pursuits can provide a healthy outlet for managing and regulating emotions.

Positive Distraction: Intellectual activities can serve as a positive distraction from negative thoughts and emotions.

Improved Problem-Solving: Intellectual stimulation can enhance problem-solving skills, helping individuals approach challenges with a more constructive mindset.

Balancing Mental Challenges with Relaxation

While intellectual self-care encourages mental stimulation, it's essential to balance mental challenges with relaxation and rest. Overloading your mind with constant stimulation can lead to burnout and stress. Here are some tips for finding balance:

Mindful Relaxation: Practice mindful relaxation techniques, such as meditation or deep breathing exercises, to unwind and de-stress.

Time Management: Allocate specific periods for intellectual pursuits and ensure you schedule downtime for relaxation and leisure.

Variety: Mix intellectual activities with enjoyable, non-demanding pastimes. This variety helps maintain balance and prevents mental fatigue.

Prioritization: Identify your intellectual interests and prioritize activities that align with your passions and goals.

Self-Reflection: Periodically assess your mental and emotional state to ensure you are striking a healthy balance between intellectual stimulation and relaxation.

4.5 Creative Self-Care

Unleashing Creativity as a Form of Self-Expression

Creative self-care taps into your innate capacity for self-expression and allows you to explore your creativity in various forms. Engaging in creative activities can be deeply fulfilling and therapeutic.

Creative Outlets: Identify creative outlets that resonate with you. This could include writing, painting, drawing, playing a musical instrument, crafting, or any other form of self-expression.

Therapeutic Benefits: Creative self-care can provide emotional release, reduce stress, and offer a sense of accomplishment. It allows you to channel your thoughts and emotions into a tangible and expressive medium.

Finding Inspiration in Everyday Life: Creativity doesn't require special circumstances or materials. You can find inspiration in everyday life, whether it's through nature, personal experiences, or the people you encounter.

The Therapeutic Benefits of Artistic Pursuits

Engaging in artistic pursuits offers therapeutic benefits that contribute to emotional well-being:

Emotional Expression: Artistic endeavors provide a safe and constructive way to express complex emotions that may be challenging to articulate verbally.

Stress Reduction: Creative activities can be relaxing and meditative, reducing stress levels and promoting a sense of calm.

Enhanced Self-Awareness: Through creative self-expression, individuals often gain insight into their emotions, thoughts, and beliefs, fostering greater self-awareness.

Sense of Accomplishment: Completing a creative project can boost self-esteem and provide a sense of accomplishment and pride.

Connection and Community: Engaging in creative hobbies can connect you with like-minded individuals and communities, fostering a sense of belonging and camaraderie.

Incorporating creative self-care into your routine allows you to tap into your inner artist, explore your passions, and find joy in the process of creation.

In conclusion, self-care is a holistic practice that encompasses various dimensions of well-being. Physical self-care ensures the body is in optimal condition to support your overall health. Emotional self-care equips you with the tools to manage your emotions and develop emotional resilience. Social self-care emphasizes the importance of healthy relationships and setting boundaries. Intellectual self-care fosters mental stimulation and lifelong learning, while creative self-care encourages self-expression and artistic exploration. By integrating these self-care practices into your life, you can nurture your mind, body, and spirit, leading to a more balanced and fulfilling existence.

Chapter 5: Overcoming Obstacles to Self-

Care

5.1 Cultural and Societal Influences

- The cultural stigma surrounding self-care.
- The glorification of busyness and its consequences.
- Shifting societal perceptions of self-care.

5.2 Time Management and Prioritization

- Strategies for carving out time for self-care.
- The importance of making self-care a priority.
- Balancing work, family, and personal needs.

5.3 Self-Care for Different Stages of Life

- Adapting self-care practices to various life stages.
- Self-care for parents, caregivers, and seniors.
- The lifelong journey of self-care.

Overcoming Obstacles to Self-Care

Self-care is a practice that holds the promise of improved well-being, but it's not always easy to prioritize in a world filled with demands and distractions. In this chapter, we will explore the obstacles that can hinder the practice of self-care and provide strategies for overcoming them. From cultural and societal influences to time management and the challenges of different life stages, we'll navigate the barriers that may stand in the way of your self-care journey.

5.1 Cultural and Societal Influences

The Cultural Stigma Surrounding Self-Care

In many cultures, there exists a stigma surrounding self-care. It is often seen as selfish or indulgent, especially when compared to the values of sacrifice and selflessness. This stigma can create barriers to prioritizing self-care in one's life.

Strategies to Overcome Cultural Stigma:

Education: Educate yourself and others about the importance of self-care for mental and physical health. Share information and resources that highlight the benefits of self-care practices.

Reframe Self-Care: Reframe self-care as a responsible act rather than a selfish one. Emphasize that taking care of your own well-being enables you to better care for others and fulfill your responsibilities.

Set Boundaries: Clearly communicate your self-care boundaries to those around you. Let them know when and how you plan to engage in self-care, so they can better understand and respect your choices.

The Glorification of Busyness and Its Consequences

Modern society often glorifies busyness as a badge of honor. Being constantly busy is seen as a symbol of productivity and success. However, this mindset can have detrimental effects on mental and physical health.

Strategies to Overcome the Glorification of Busyness:

Mindful Awareness: Practice mindful awareness of your schedule and commitments. Reflect on whether your busyness is aligned with your values and well-being.

Prioritize Self-Care: Recognize that self-care is a vital component of overall health. Prioritize it alongside work and other responsibilities.

Set Realistic Expectations: Avoid overcommitting and set realistic expectations for your workload. Learning to say "No" when necessary is a crucial aspect of self-care.

Shifting Societal Perceptions of Self-Care

Societal perceptions of self-care are evolving. There is a growing recognition of the importance of self-care for mental health and well-being. However, it's essential to continue shifting these perceptions to create a culture that values and supports self-care.

Strategies to Promote Shifting Perceptions:

Advocate for Change: Be an advocate for self-care in your community and workplace. Share your experiences and encourage others to prioritize self-care.

Supportive Communities: Seek out and create communities that emphasize self-care. Surrounding yourself with like-minded individuals can provide validation and motivation.

Lead by Example: Demonstrate the positive effects of self-care in your own life. When others witness the benefits, they may be more inclined to prioritize self-care themselves.

5.2 Time Management and Prioritization

Strategies for Carving Out Time for Self-Care

Time management is a common obstacle to self-care. Many people struggle to find time in their busy schedules to dedicate to self-care practices. However, with effective time management strategies, it's possible to make self-care a regular part of your routine.

Strategies for Carving Out Time:

Schedule Self-Care: Treat self-care activities as appointments on your calendar. Designate specific times for self-care, whether it's daily, weekly, or monthly.

Start Small: Begin with small, manageable self-care practices that can be integrated into your existing schedule. As you experience the benefits, you may be more motivated to allocate more time.

Eliminate Time-Wasters: Identify and minimize time-wasting activities in your daily life, such as excessive social media use or procrastination. Redirect that time toward self-care.

Delegate Tasks: Delegate tasks and responsibilities when possible. Sharing the load with others allows you to free up time for self-care.

Prioritize Self-Care: Make self-care a non-negotiable priority. Recognize that taking care of your well-being is essential for overall health and productivity.

The Importance of Making Self-Care a Priority

Prioritizing self-care is a mindset shift that can significantly impact your well-being. When self-care becomes a non-negotiable aspect of your life, you are more likely to overcome time management challenges and other obstacles.

Benefits of Prioritizing Self-Care:

Improved Well-Being: Prioritizing self-care leads to improved physical and mental well-being, allowing you to perform better in all areas of your life.

Resilience: Self-care enhances your ability to cope with stress and challenges, making you more resilient in the face of adversity.

Productivity: Taking breaks for self-care can boost your productivity and creativity, ultimately saving you time in the long run.

Prevent Burnout: Prioritizing self-care is a proactive measure to prevent burnout, which can have long-lasting negative consequences.

5.3 Self-Care for Different Stages of Life

Adapting Self-Care Practices to Various Life Stages

Self-care is not a one-size-fits-all practice; it needs to adapt to different stages of life. Whether you are a parent, caregiver, or senior, the self-care practices that work best for you may change over time.

Adapting Self-Care Practices:

Parents: Parents often have limited time for self-care, so it's essential to focus on efficient and practical self-care practices. These might include short mindfulness exercises, quick workouts, or self-compassion techniques.

Caregivers: Caregivers face unique challenges, including high levels of stress and emotional strain. Self-care for caregivers may involve seeking support from support groups, respite care, and utilizing available resources for assistance.

Seniors: As individuals age, their self-care needs may shift toward maintaining physical and cognitive health. Activities such as gentle exercise, brain games, and social engagement become important.

The Lifelong Journey of Self-Care

Self-care is not a destination but a lifelong journey. It evolves alongside your changing needs and circumstances. Embrace the evolving nature of self-care and be open to adjusting your self-care practices as you progress through life.

Keys to a Lifelong Self-Care Journey:

Flexibility: Be flexible and adaptable in your self-care practices. Recognize that what works best for you may change over time.

Self-Reflection: Regularly assess your well-being and needs. Self-reflection allows you to stay attuned to your changing requirements for self-care.

Seek Guidance: If you're uncertain about the most appropriate self-care practices for your current life stage, seek guidance from healthcare professionals, therapists, or support groups.

Celebrate Progress: Celebrate your self-care milestones and successes along the way. Acknowledge the positive impact that self-care has had on your life.

In conclusion, overcoming obstacles to self-care is an essential aspect of maintaining overall well-being. Cultural and societal influences, the glorification of busyness, and shifting perceptions of self-care can impact your ability to prioritize self-care. Effective time management and the prioritization of self-care are crucial steps in overcoming these obstacles. Additionally, self-care needs to adapt to different stages of life, and recognizing the evolving nature of self-care is key to maintaining a lifelong self-care journey. By addressing these challenges and implementing strategies for overcoming them, you can unlock the full potential of self-care and reap its many benefits.

Chapter 6: The Science of Self-Care

6.1 The Neurobiology of Self-Care

- How self-care affects the brain's reward system.
- Neurotransmitters and hormones involved in self-care.
- The role of neuroplasticity in self-care practices.

6.2 Self-Care and Physical Health

- The impact of self-care on immune function.
- The connection between self-care and chronic diseases.
- The role of inflammation in health and self-care.

The Science of Self-Care

Self-care is more than just a feel-good practice; it has a profound impact on your physical and mental well-being. In this chapter, we'll explore the science behind self-care, shedding light on the neurobiology of self-care and its role in physical health. Understanding the science of self-care can empower you to make informed choices and prioritize self-care practices that support your overall health and vitality.

6.1 The Neurobiology of Self-Care

How Self-Care Affects the Brain's Reward System

Self-care activities, such as relaxation, exercise, and engaging in pleasurable experiences, activate the brain's reward system. This system is responsible for the release of neurotransmitters like dopamine, which are associated with feelings of pleasure and reward.

Dopamine Release: Engaging in self-care practices triggers the release of dopamine in the brain. This release reinforces the behavior, making it more likely that you'll repeat self-care activities.

Positive Reinforcement: The brain associates self-care with positive feelings, creating a positive feedback loop. Over time, this can lead to a stronger inclination to prioritize self-care.

Stress Reduction: Self-care practices also reduce the production of stress hormones like cortisol. Lower stress levels contribute to better overall mental and physical health.

Neurotransmitters and Hormones Involved in Self-Care

Self-care practices influence various neurotransmitters and hormones that play critical roles in regulating mood, stress, and overall well-being.

Serotonin: Self-care activities like exercise and exposure to natural light can boost serotonin levels. Serotonin is a neurotransmitter associated with mood regulation and feelings of well-being.

Endorphins: Physical activities, especially those that are enjoyable, release endorphins. Endorphins are natural painkillers and mood elevators that promote feelings of happiness and relaxation.

Oxytocin: Social self-care, such as spending time with loved ones or engaging in acts of kindness, triggers the release of oxytocin. This hormone is known as the "bonding hormone" and promotes social connection and emotional bonding.

Cortisol: Effective stress management through self-care practices reduces cortisol levels. High cortisol levels are associated with chronic stress and its adverse effects on health.

The Role of Neuroplasticity in Self-Care Practices

Neuroplasticity refers to the brain's ability to reorganize and adapt by forming new neural connections throughout life. Self-care practices have been shown to enhance neuroplasticity, promoting cognitive flexibility, learning, and emotional resilience.

Mental Stimulation: Intellectual self-care, which includes activities like reading, learning, and problem-solving, stimulates brain regions associated with memory and cognitive function. This stimulation supports the brain's plasticity.

Mindfulness and Meditation: Mindfulness practices, a common form of self-care, have been shown to enhance neuroplasticity. These practices encourage present-moment awareness and foster changes in the brain's structure and function.

Emotional Regulation: Emotional self-care, including strategies like relaxation and mindfulness, can positively impact emotional regulation by rewiring neural pathways associated with stress and reactivity.

6.2 Self-Care and Physical Health

The Impact of Self-Care on Immune Function

Self-care practices have a direct impact on immune function. Chronic stress, which can result from neglecting self-care, weakens the immune system and makes the body more susceptible to infections and diseases.

Stress Reduction: Engaging in self-care activities that reduce stress levels, such as meditation, relaxation, and exercise, helps support a healthy immune system.

Enhanced Immune Response: Self-care practices can enhance the immune response by reducing inflammation and promoting the production of immune cells that defend the body against pathogens.

Balanced Immune Function: Self-care practices contribute to immune homeostasis, ensuring that the immune system functions neither overreactively (causing autoimmune conditions) nor underreactively (leaving the body vulnerable to infections).

The Connection Between Self-Care and Chronic Diseases

Chronic diseases, such as cardiovascular disease, diabetes, and autoimmune disorders, are often influenced by lifestyle factors, including self-care practices.

Prevention and Management: Self-care practices, particularly those related to diet, exercise, and stress management, are instrumental in preventing and managing chronic diseases.

Inflammation Control: Chronic inflammation is a common factor in many chronic diseases. Self-care practices that reduce inflammation, such as a balanced diet and regular exercise, can mitigate disease progression.

Mental Health: Mental health is intricately linked to physical health. Self-care practices that address mental well-being, like therapy and stress reduction, can improve outcomes for chronic diseases.

The Role of Inflammation in Health and Self-Care

Inflammation is a natural response of the immune system to injury or infection. However, chronic inflammation, often driven by poor lifestyle choices and stress, can contribute to the development of various health problems.

Inflammation and Disease: Chronic inflammation has been linked to the development of numerous diseases, including heart disease, diabetes, cancer, and autoimmune disorders.

Inflammation and Aging: Chronic inflammation also accelerates the aging process and is associated with age-related diseases. Self-care practices that reduce inflammation can promote healthy aging.

Self-Care for Inflammation Control: Several self-care practices can help control inflammation, including a balanced diet rich in anti-inflammatory foods (e.g., fruits and vegetables), regular physical activity, stress management, and quality sleep.

In conclusion, the science of self-care reveals the intricate connections between self-care practices, the brain's reward system, neurotransmitters, hormones, and physical health. Engaging in self-care triggers the release of feel-good neurotransmitters, reduces stress hormones, and enhances neuroplasticity. Moreover, self-care practices have a profound impact on immune function, chronic disease prevention, and inflammation control. By understanding the scientific basis of self-care, individuals can make informed choices to prioritize self-care practices that support their overall well-being and vitality.

Chapter 7: Self-Care as a Global Movement

7.1 Cultural Variations in Self-Care

- Examining self-care practices across different cultures.
- The universality of self-care principles.
- Cultural influences on self-care perceptions.

7.2 The Role of Technology in Self-Care

- The influence of digital tools and apps on self-care.
- How technology can both help and hinder self-care efforts.
- Ethical considerations in the digital self-care landscape.

Self-Care as a Global Movement

Self-care is a universal concept that transcends cultural boundaries. It encompasses practices that promote physical, mental, and emotional well-being, and its principles are applicable to people across the globe. In this chapter, we will explore the cultural variations in self-care practices and the role of technology in shaping and influencing the global self-care movement.

7.1 Cultural Variations in Self-Care

Examining Self-Care Practices Across Different Cultures

Self-care practices can vary significantly from one culture to another, influenced by traditions, beliefs, and social norms. While the specific methods and rituals may differ, the fundamental principles of self-care remain constant—nurturing one's physical, mental, and emotional health.

Cultural Practices: In some cultures, self-care may involve traditional healing modalities like Ayurveda in India, acupuncture in China, or mindfulness practices rooted in Buddhist traditions. These practices have deep historical and cultural significance.

Dietary Choices: Food plays a crucial role in self-care across cultures. Mediterranean diets emphasize fresh vegetables and olive oil, while Asian cultures incorporate rice, fish, and various fermented foods. These dietary choices reflect cultural values and nutritional wisdom.

Mindfulness and Meditation: Mindfulness and meditation, though rooted in various cultural contexts (e.g., Zen Buddhism in Japan, and Vipassana in India), have gained global popularity. These practices highlight the universal need for mental and emotional well-being.

The Universality of Self-Care Principles

While specific self-care practices may vary, the core principles of self-care—prioritizing one's well-being, managing stress, seeking balance, and fostering resilience—are universally applicable. These principles resonate with people from diverse backgrounds because they address fundamental human needs.

Stress Management: Every culture experiences stress, and the need to manage it is universal. Whether through yoga, tai chi, or deep breathing exercises, people worldwide seek ways to alleviate stress.

Physical Activity: The importance of physical activity for health is a global consensus. While the types of physical activities may differ (e.g., yoga in India, and soccer in Brazil), the pursuit of an active lifestyle is a common goal.

Mental and Emotional Health: The acknowledgment of mental and emotional health as integral to overall well-being is a shared belief. Accessible mental health resources and support are essential in all cultures.

Cultural Influences on Self-Care Perceptions

Cultural factors significantly shape how self-care is perceived and practiced. Understanding these influences is vital for promoting culturally sensitive and inclusive self-care approaches.

Collectivism vs. Individualism: Cultures that prioritize collectivism may emphasize communal well-being over individual self-care. In contrast, individualistic cultures often prioritize personal autonomy and self-care practices.

Spirituality and Religion: Many self-care practices are deeply intertwined with spirituality and religion. In cultures where spirituality plays a central role, self-care may involve prayer, meditation, or rituals that promote spiritual growth.

Stigma and Taboos: Cultural taboos and stigma surrounding mental health can deter individuals from seeking help or openly discussing self-care. Raising awareness and reducing stigma are critical steps in promoting self-care in such cultures.

7.2 The Role of Technology in Self-Care

The Influence of Digital Tools and Apps on Self-Care

Advancements in technology have significantly impacted the self-care landscape. Digital tools and mobile apps have made self-care practices more accessible and personalized.

Wellness Apps: There is an abundance of wellness apps that offer guided meditation, exercise routines, sleep tracking, and mental health support. These apps make self-care practices convenient and tailored to individual needs.

Wearable Devices: Wearable technology like fitness trackers and smartwatches has enabled individuals to monitor their physical activity, sleep patterns, and stress levels in real-time. These devices promote self-awareness and accountability.

Telehealth and Online Therapy: The rise of telehealth and online therapy platforms has expanded access to mental health care, especially in areas with limited resources. Virtual sessions facilitate therapy and counseling, enhancing mental health self-care.

How Technology Can Both Help and Hinder Self-Care Efforts

While technology offers numerous benefits for self-care, it can also present challenges and potential drawbacks.

Digital Overload: Excessive screen time and digital distractions can contribute to stress and detract from self-care efforts. Striking a balance between using technology for self-care and disconnecting from it is essential.

Privacy and Data Security: Using digital tools and apps often involves sharing personal data. Ensuring data privacy and security is critical to maintaining trust in digital self-care solutions.

Technological Barriers: Not everyone has equal access to technology or the digital literacy needed to use self-care apps effectively. These barriers can exacerbate health disparities.

Ethical Considerations in the Digital Self-Care Landscape

As the digital self-care landscape continues to evolve, ethical considerations become increasingly important.

Informed Consent: Users of self-care apps should be well-informed about data collection practices, privacy policies, and how their information will be used. Informed consent ensures users are aware of the implications of using digital tools.

Data Ownership: Users should have control over their data and the ability to delete or export it as they wish. Transparent data ownership policies empower individuals to make informed choices.

Accessibility and Inclusivity: Developers of self-care apps should prioritize accessibility and inclusivity to ensure that their products are usable by people with disabilities and from diverse cultural backgrounds.

In conclusion, self-care is a global movement that transcends cultural boundaries. While specific self-care practices may vary across cultures, the core principles of well-being, stress management, and resilience are universally applicable. The role of technology in self-care is significant, offering both opportunities and challenges. Digital tools and apps can make self-care more accessible but require ethical considerations regarding privacy, data ownership, and inclusivity. Understanding cultural variations in self-care practices and navigating the digital self-care landscape are essential steps in promoting well-being on a global scale.

Chapter 8: Self-Care for a Sustainable Future

8.1 Self-Care and Environmental Consciousness

- How self-care can promote environmental awareness.
- Sustainable self-care practices for a healthier planet.
- The connection between nature and well-being.

8.2 Self-Care in the Workplace

- The importance of self-care in professional settings.
- Creating a culture of self-care in organizations.
- The economic benefits of a self-care-aware workforce.

Self-Care for a Sustainable Future

In an increasingly interconnected world, self-care takes on new dimensions beyond individual well-being. It has the power to impact not only our personal lives but also the environment and workplaces we inhabit. In this chapter, we explore the role of self-care in promoting environmental consciousness and its importance in the workplace for a sustainable future.

8.1 Self-Care and Environmental Consciousness

How Self-Care Can Promote Environmental Awareness

Self-care practices often involve spending time outdoors, reconnecting with nature, and cultivating mindfulness. These activities can foster a deeper connection to the environment and increase environmental awareness.

Nature as a Source of Healing: Time spent in natural settings has been shown to reduce stress, improve mood, and enhance overall well-being. As individuals experience the healing effects of nature, they may become more inclined to protect it.

Mindfulness and Sustainability: Mindfulness practices, which are often part of self-care routines, encourage present-moment awareness. This heightened awareness can extend to environmental concerns, prompting individuals to make more sustainable choices in their daily lives.

Eco-Therapy: Eco-therapy is a form of therapy that incorporates outdoor and nature-based activities. It emphasizes the healing power of nature and encourages individuals to connect with and protect the environment.

Sustainable Self-Care Practices for a Healthier Planet

Self-care and environmental sustainability can go hand in hand. Individuals can adopt sustainable self-care practices that benefit both their well-being and the planet.

Eco-Friendly Products: Using eco-friendly self-care products, such as natural skincare items and reusable toiletries, reduces the environmental impact of personal care routines.

Mindful Consumption: Practicing mindful consumption involves making intentional choices about the products you purchase and the resources you use. This can reduce waste and support sustainable practices.

Green Spaces: Seek out green spaces and natural environments for self-care activities like hiking, picnicking, or simply enjoying the outdoors. These experiences deepen your connection to nature.

The Connection Between Nature and Well-Being

Numerous studies have highlighted the positive impact of nature on well-being. Spending time in natural settings can lead to physical, mental, and emotional benefits.

Stress Reduction: Nature has a calming effect on the mind and can reduce stress levels. The presence of green spaces has been linked to lower cortisol levels, the hormone associated with stress.

Improved Mood: Exposure to natural environments has been shown to improve mood and reduce symptoms of anxiety and depression. Nature provides a sense of peace and tranquility that can boost mental well-being.

Physical Health: Outdoor activities like walking, hiking, and gardening promote physical health. These activities encourage exercise, which is essential for overall well-being.

8.2 Self-Care in the Workplace

The Importance of Self-Care in Professional Settings

Self-care is not limited to personal lives; it also plays a crucial role in professional settings. Individuals who practice self-care are more likely to be productive, engaged, and satisfied in their work.

Burnout Prevention: Self-care practices help prevent burnout, a prevalent issue in the workplace. Burnout can lead to decreased job satisfaction, productivity, and overall well-being.

Enhanced Focus and Creativity: Regular self-care activities, such as mindfulness and stress reduction techniques, can enhance focus, creativity, and problem-solving abilities, which are valuable in the workplace.

Work-Life Balance: Self-care encourages individuals to maintain a healthy work-life balance. This balance fosters greater job satisfaction and reduces the risk of work-related stress.

Creating a Culture of Self-Care in Organizations

Organizations have a role to play in promoting self-care among their employees. Cultivating a culture of self-care can lead to a more engaged and healthier workforce.

Supportive Policies: Employers can implement policies that support work-life balance, flexible schedules, and mental health resources. These policies demonstrate a commitment to employee well-being.

Mental Health Resources: Providing access to mental health resources, including counseling and stress management programs, can help employees address mental health challenges.

Wellness Programs: Wellness programs that incorporate self-care practices, such as yoga classes, mindfulness training, and exercise facilities, can encourage healthy habits among employees.

The Economic Benefits of a Self-Care-Aware Workforce

Investing in self-care among employees can yield significant economic benefits for organizations. A self-care-aware workforce is more productive, engaged, and likely to contribute to a company's success.

Reduced Absenteeism: Self-care practices can reduce the occurrence of physical and mental health issues that lead to absenteeism. Employees who prioritize self-care are less likely to take sick days.

Increased Productivity: Engaging in self-care can enhance focus, creativity, and problem-solving abilities, leading to increased productivity and efficiency in the workplace.

Lower Healthcare Costs: A self-care-aware workforce is generally healthier, leading to lower healthcare costs for organizations. Preventing health issues through self-care reduces the need for medical interventions.

Improved Employee Retention: Employees who feel supported in their self-care efforts are more likely to stay with an organization, reducing turnover and associated hiring costs.

In conclusion, self-care is a multifaceted concept that extends beyond individual well-being. It can promote environmental consciousness by fostering a deeper connection to nature and encouraging sustainable practices. In the workplace, self-care is essential for preventing burnout, enhancing productivity, and creating a culture of well-being. Organizations that prioritize self-care among employees stand to benefit economically through reduced absenteeism, increased productivity, and improved employee retention. Embracing self-care for a sustainable future means recognizing its far-reaching impact on individuals, communities, and the planet as a whole.

Conclusion

"I can't handle me in any kind of way" need not be a lamentation; it can be a catalyst for positive change. In this comprehensive exploration of self-care, we have seen how it is not a selfish act but a fundamental necessity for a fulfilling life. Integrating self-care into our daily routines, prioritizing our well-being, and recognizing the interconnectedness of mind, body, and spirit can lead to a profound transformation. As we move forward in our journey toward self-care, we not only enhance our individual lives but also contribute to a more compassionate and sustainable world.

Throughout this book, we've embarked on a journey through the multifaceted landscape of self-care. We've delved into its various dimensions, from understanding its essence to exploring its impact on our mental, physical, and spiritual well-being. We've examined the science behind self-care, showcasing the intricate relationship between our neurobiology, physical health, and self-care practices. We've also discussed how self-care transcends individual boundaries, becoming a global movement that encompasses diverse cultures and technological advances.

One of the core messages that emerges from our exploration is that self-care is not a luxury but a fundamental right and a responsibility. It's a conscious choice to prioritize our well-being, recognizing that by nurturing ourselves, we become better equipped to navigate life's challenges and support those around us. Self-care is not a one-size-fits-all solution; it's a deeply personal journey where we must discover what practices resonate with us and bring us closer to balance and harmony.

In the realm of the mind, we've learned about the intricate dance between mental and physical health. Stress, a common companion in our lives, can wreak havoc on both our minds and bodies. Self-care practices provide the tools to reduce stress, enhance our resilience, and promote emotional well-being. From mindfulness and meditation to emotional self-care and the importance of seeking support, we've explored a myriad of strategies to nurture our mental health.

Moving into the physical domain, we've recognized the significance of taking care of our bodies. Exercise, nutrition, and sleep are the cornerstones of physical self-care, each contributing to our overall vitality. Overcoming the barriers that hinder our physical well-being, from time constraints to lifestyle choices, is a critical step in the journey of self-care. As we nourish our bodies, we enhance our energy, strength, and longevity.

Social self-care has underscored the importance of our relationships and the need to set boundaries that protect our well-being. Building healthy connections and fostering a support system can significantly impact our mental health. We've seen that self-care is not a solitary endeavor; it thrives in the company of kindred spirits who share our commitment to well-being.

Intellectual self-care has championed continuous learning as a means to nourish our minds. It's through intellectual stimulation that we can not only expand our knowledge but also enhance our emotional well-being. Balancing mental challenges with relaxation and mindfulness is the key to intellectual self-care.

Creative self-care has celebrated the therapeutic benefits of artistic expression and the inspiration found in everyday life. Unleashing our creativity is a form of self-expression that feeds our souls and allows us to tap into the profound joy of being in the moment.

Our exploration hasn't been limited to personal practices; we've also encountered obstacles on our path to self-care. Cultural and societal influences often stigmatize self-care, glorify busyness, and shape our perceptions of this essential practice. We've learned to navigate these challenges, carve out time for self-care, and adapt self-care practices to different stages of life.

We've also recognized that self-care extends beyond the individual and contributes to a global movement. Cultural variations in self-care practices enrich our understanding of its universality and cultural influences. Technology, with its myriad apps and digital tools, has made self-care more accessible, but it also raises ethical considerations that require our attention and scrutiny.

As we conclude this journey through the world of self-care, it's clear that self-care is not a solitary act but a collective endeavor. It's a commitment to ourselves, our communities, and our planet. It's a recognition that our well-being is intricately linked to the well-being of the world around us. When we prioritize self-care, we become better equipped to address the challenges and opportunities that life presents. We become more compassionate, resilient, and capable of contributing to a more compassionate and sustainable world.

In the midst of our fast-paced lives, we must pause, reflect, and remember that taking care of ourselves is not selfish; it's an act of profound wisdom and self-compassion. It's an affirmation that we are worthy of love, care, and attention. As we continue on our journey of self-care, may we carry with us the knowledge that we are not alone. We are part of a global community that recognizes the transformative power of self-care. Together, we can create a world where well-being is cherished, where self-care is celebrated, and where the mind, body, and spirit thrive in harmony.

From The Author

As we conclude this exploration of self-care, I want to offer my sincere thanks for joining me on this transformative journey. Remember that self-care is a lifelong practice, a continuous commitment to your well-being. Embrace it with compassion and patience, and don't be discouraged by setbacks. Your well-being matters and your journey is unique. Continue to prioritize self-care, for in doing so, you not only enrich your own life but also radiate positivity and well-being to the world around you. Together, we can create a more compassionate, resilient, and sustainable future. Keep nurturing your mind, body, and spirit. You've got this!

Made in the USA
Columbia, SC
10 June 2024

36439454R00052